First World War
and Army of Occupation
War Diary
France, Belgium and Germany

66 DIVISION
197 Infantry Brigade
202 Machine Gun Company
10 February 1917 - 28 February 1918

WO95/3137/3

The Naval & Military Press Ltd
www.nmarchive.com
Published in association with The National Archives

Published by

The Naval & Military Press Ltd

Unit 10 Ridgewood Industrial Park,

Uckfield, East Sussex,

TN22 5QE England

Tel: +44 (0) 1825 749494

www.naval-military-press.com

www.nmarchive.com

This diary has been reprinted in facsimile from the original. Any imperfections are inevitably reproduced and the quality may fall short of modern type and cartographic standards.

© **Crown Copyright**
Images reproduced by permission of The National Archives, London, England, 2015.

Contents

Document type	Place/Title	Date From	Date To
Heading	WO95/3137/3		
Heading	66th Division 197th Infy Bde 202nd Machine Gun Coy Mar 1917-Feb 1918		
Heading	197th Brigade 66th Division Disembarked Havre 5.3.17. 202nd Machine Gun Company March 1917.		
War Diary	Belton Park	04/10/1917	04/10/1917
War Diary	Grantham	10/02/1917	10/02/1917
War Diary	Fovant Camp	10/02/1917	04/03/1917
War Diary	Southamton	04/03/1917	04/03/1917
War Diary	Le Havre	05/03/1917	13/03/1917
War Diary	Abbeville	14/03/1917	14/03/1917
War Diary	Chocques	14/03/1917	14/03/1917
War Diary	Bethune	15/03/1917	16/03/1917
War Diary	Gorre	16/03/1917	16/03/1917
War Diary	Givenchy And Festubert Sectors	16/03/1917	31/03/1917
Heading	197th Brigade 66th Division 202nd Machine Gun Company April 1917.		
War Diary	Givenchy And Festubert Sectors	01/04/1917	30/04/1917
Heading	197th Brigade 66th Division 202nd Machine Gun Company May 1917.		
War Diary	Givenchy And Festubert Sectors	01/05/1917	31/05/1917
Heading	197th Brigade 66th Division 202nd Machine Gun Company June 1917		
War Diary	Givenchy And Festubert Sectors	01/06/1917	20/06/1917
War Diary	Bellerive Bethune Combined Sheet Edit 6	21/06/1917	24/06/1917
War Diary	Dunkerque	25/06/1917	30/06/1917
Heading	197th Brigade 66th Division 202nd Machine Gun Company July 1917.		
Heading	War Diary of 202nd M.G. Coy From July 1st 1917 To July 31st 1917 (Volume 5)		
War Diary	Teteghem C 9 A 40 40	01/07/1917	09/07/1917
War Diary	Leffrin Chouke C 5a 50.55	10/07/1917	11/07/1917
War Diary	Nieuport Bains Sector	11/07/1917	31/07/1917
Heading	197th Brigade. 66th Division 202nd Machine Gun Company August 1917.		
Heading	War Diary of 202nd Machine Gun Company From Aug 1st 1917 to Aug 31st 1917 Volume 6		
War Diary	Surrey Camp R 32 A	01/08/1917	10/08/1917
War Diary	Surrey Camp	11/08/1917	15/08/1917
War Diary	Surrey Camp R 32 A	16/08/1917	19/08/1917
War Diary	Nieuport Bains Sector	20/08/1917	31/08/1917
Heading	197th Brigade. 66th Division. 202nd Machine Gun Company September 1917		
Heading	War Diary of 202 Machine Gun Company. From:- 1st September 1917. To:- 30th. September 1917 Volume 8.		
War Diary	Nieuport Bains Sector	01/09/1917	04/09/1917
War Diary	Surrey Camp R 32 A	05/09/1917	13/09/1917
War Diary	Nieuport Bains Sector	14/09/1917	23/09/1917
War Diary	Bray Dunes	24/09/1917	25/09/1917
War Diary	Arques	26/09/1917	30/09/1917

Operation(al) Order(s)	202nd M.G. Coy Operation Order No 30		
Miscellaneous	Appendix "A" Right Sub-Sector	03/07/1917	03/07/1917
Miscellaneous	Appendix 'B' Left Sub Sector & H.Q	03/09/1917	03/09/1917
Heading	197th Brigade. 66th Division. 202nd Machine Gun Company October 1917		
Heading	War Diary of 202nd M.G. Coy From 1.10.1917-31.10.17 (Volume 8)		
War Diary	Arques S 15c 70 80 Aecke Area	01/10/1917	04/10/1917
War Diary	Winnezeele Area	05/10/1917	05/10/1917
War Diary	Zonnebeke Sector	06/10/1917	11/10/1917
War Diary	Winnezeele Area	12/10/1917	20/10/1917
War Diary	Renescure Area	21/10/1917	31/10/1917
Operation(al) Order(s)	Operation Order No 37 by Captain G.E. Gilbert M.C. Commanding 202 M.G.Coy	08/10/1917	08/10/1917
Heading	197th Brigade. 66th Division. 202nd Machine Gun Company November 1917.		
Heading	War Diary of 202 Machine Gun Coy From 1.11.1917 To 30.11.17 Volume 9		
War Diary	Renescure Area	01/11/1917	07/11/1917
War Diary	West Outre Area	08/11/1917	08/11/1917
War Diary	Ypres Sector	09/11/1917	09/11/1917
War Diary	Zonnebeke Sector	09/11/1917	24/11/1917
War Diary	Berthen Area	25/11/1917	25/11/1917
War Diary	Staple Area	26/11/1917	26/11/1917
Heading	197th Brigade.66th Division 202nd Machine Gun Company December 1917.		
Heading	War Diary of 202nd Machine Gun Company From 1.12.17 To 31.12.17 Volume 10		
War Diary	Staple Area	01/12/1917	31/12/1917
Heading	202 Machine Gun Company Jan 1918		
War Diary	Staple Area	01/01/1918	10/01/1918
War Diary	Canal Area & Zonnebeke Sector	11/01/1918	31/01/1918
Heading	War Diary of 202 Machine Gun Coy From Feb 1st To Feb 28th 1918		
War Diary	Zonnebeke Sector & Canal Area	01/02/1918	10/02/1918
War Diary	Proven Area	10/02/1918	16/02/1918
War Diary	Guillaucourt	17/02/1918	28/02/1918

WO 95/3137/3

66TH DIVISION
197TH INFY BDE

202ND MACHINE GUN COY.
MAR 1917-FEB 1918

197th Brigade.
66th Division.

Disembarked HAVRE 5.3.17.

202nd MACHINE GUN COMPANY MARCH 1917.

Army Form C. 2118.

WAR DIARY
or
INTELLIGENCE SUMMARY.

202 MACHINE GUN COMPANY

Vol 1 #1

Place	Date	Hour	Summary of Events and Information	Remarks and references to Appendices
BELTON PARK	1.2.10.17		Mobilizing and training	
GRANTHAM	10.2.17		Awaiting orders to proceed overseas	
FOVANT CAMP	12.2.17			
- do -	4.3.17	7.25 AM	Entrained for SOUTHAMPTON	
SOUTHAMPTON	4.3.17	8.30 PM	Embarked for FRANCE on S/s ARCHANGEL	
LE HAVRE	5.3.17	8.30 AM	Disembarked and marched to No 1 LARGE REST CAMP	
- do -	13.3.17	3.30 PM	Paraded and marched to GARE DE MARCHANDISES	
- do -	13.3.17	3.39 PM		
- do -	13.3.17	5.0 PM	Entrained at GARE DE MARCHANDISES	
ABBEVILLE	14.3.17	10 AM	Halted for 45 minutes	
CHOCQUES	14.3.17	7 PM	Detrained and marched BETHUNE	
BETHUNE	15.3.17	2 AM	Proceeded to trenches in GIVENCHY and FESTUBERT SECTORS and carried out a reconnaissance of MACHINE GUN POSITIONS with O.C. 13th MACHINE GUN COY	
BETHUNE	16.3.17	8.30 AM	Company marched to GORRE	
GORRE	16.3.17	10 AM	Took over duties from 13th MACHINE GUN COY	
GIVENCHY AND FESTUBERT SECTORS	16.3.17	11 AM	Took over MACHINE GUN POSITIONS from 13th MACHINE GUN COY	

Original

Shrurr.02

Army Form C. 2118.

Instructions regarding War Diaries and Intelligence
Summaries are contained in F. S. Regs., Part II,
and the Staff Manual respectively. Title pages
will be prepared in manuscript.

WAR DIARY
or
INTELLIGENCE SUMMARY.
(Erase heading not required.)

202nd MACHINE GUN COMPANY

Place	Date	Hour	Summary of Events and Information	Remarks and references to Appendices
GIVENCHY, FESTUBERT SECTORS				
GIVENCHY	17.3.17	10.45 am	Considerable enemy Artillery and Trench Mortar activity, No damage done to Machine Gun Positions.	
G.F. SECTOR	18.3.17	3 am & 3.30 pm	Situation in general – very quiet	
- do -	19.3.17	"	Situation – quite normal	
- do -	20.3.17	"	Situation in General – normal – one man wounded and killed	
- do -			to CASUALTY CLEARING STATION, BETHUNE	
- do -	21.3.17	"	Situation – quite normal. 2nd Lieut R.N. Goode rd mattera 33 Casualty Clearing Station, BETHUNE, suffering from trenchitis	
- do -	22.3.17	"	Situation – normal. No hostile aeroplane arrived over our line during the afternoon, flying fairly low. During the day several H.E. shells fell in the vicinity of COMPANY H.Q. at GORRE. No damage done to Company billets. Saw to foot gas was passed round at 10.50 pm but the other was cancelled almost immediately	
- do -	23.3.17	"	Situation in General – normal.	
- do -	24.3.17	"	Situation in General – normal	
- do -	25.3.17	"	Situation in General – normal	

Army Form C. 2118.

Sheet No 3

WAR DIARY
or
INTELLIGENCE SUMMARY.

(Erase heading not required.)

202ⁿᵈ MACHINE GUN COMPANY

Original

Instructions regarding War Diaries and Intelligence Summaries are contained in F.S. Regs., Part II. and the Staff Manual respectively. Title pages will be prepared in manuscript.

Place	Date	Hour	Summary of Events and Information	Remarks and references to Appendices
GIVENCHY & FESTUBERT SECTORS				
G.S. SECTORS	26.3.17	3am & 3pm	Situation in general – Quiet	
- do -	27.3.17	"	Situation – normal. 2/Lt. F. BARBER reported and was taken on the strength of the Company	
- do -	28.3.17	"	Situation in general – Quite normal	
- do -	29.3.17	"	Situation in general – normal	
- do -	30.3.17	"	Situation in general – normal	
- do -	31.3.17	"	Situation in general – Quite normal	

John Ritchie Capt.

Captg. No. 202 Machine Gun Coy.

197th Brigade.
66th Division.

202nd MACHINE GUN COMPANY APRIL 1917.

MAPS. LA BASSEE 36A NW1 Béthune 8A
RICHEBOURGH 36SW3 Béthune 8A

Army Form C. 2118.

WAR DIARY
or
INTELLIGENCE SUMMARY

(Erase heading not required.)

202nd MACHINE GUN COMPANY

Vol 2

Instructions regarding War Diaries and Intelligence Summaries are contained in F. S. Regs., Part II. and the Staff Manual respectively. Title Pages will be prepared in manuscript.

Place	Date	Hour	Summary of Events and Information	Remarks and references to Appendices
GIVENCHY AND FESTUBERT SECTORS	1.4.17	8 AM	Strength of Company officers 10 other ranks 178	
do	2.4.17	-do-	Situation in General — Normal	
do	3.4.17	-do-	Situation in General — Normal	
do	4.4.17	-do-	Situation in General — Normal	
do	5.4.17	-do-	Situation in General — Normal	
do	6.4.17	-do-	Situation in General — Normal	
do	7.4.17	-do-	Situation in General — Normal	
do	8.4.17	-do-	Situation in General — Normal	
do	9.4.17	-do-	Situation in General — Normal	
do	10.4.17	-do-	Situation in General — Normal	
do	11.4.17	-do-	Situation in General — Normal	
do	12.4.17	-do-	Situation in General — Normal	

2449 Wt. W14957/Mgo 750,000 1/16 J.B.C. & A. Forms/C.2118/12.

MAPS LA BASSEE 36c NW1 Eaton 8A
RICHEBOURGH 36 SW3 Eaton 8A

Army Form C. 2118.

WAR DIARY
or
INTELLIGENCE SUMMARY

(Erase heading not required.)

202 MACHINE GUN COMPANY

Place	Date	Hour	Summary of Events and Information	Remarks and references to Appendices
GIVENCHY and FESTUBERT SECTORS	13.4.17	8 AM to 8 AM	Hostile Artillery shelled M.G. Position at S27a 8/3. No damage done to emplacement. Situation in general - Normal	
do	14.4.17	do	2 of our M.Gs. fired indirect on enemy's cross roads and communication trenches. Situation - Normal	
do	15.4.17	9 pm to 11 pm	Four of our M.Gs carried out an indirect fire scheme on enemy's communication trenches and back areas. Situation - Normal	
do	16.4.17	8.30 pm to 11.30 pm	5 Guns fired indirect on enemy's support and reserve lines	
do	17.4.17	9 pm to 11.30 pm	3 Guns fired indirect on enemy's communication trenches and Battalion H.Q. Two hostile aeroplanes attempting to cross our lines were fired upon by our M.Gs.	
do	18.4.17	8.30 pm to 11 pm	4 Guns were engaged in spraying fire to hear on enemy's support trenches, cross roads and PUMPING Stations	
do	19.4.17	9 pm to Midnight	4 Guns fired indirect on points where enemy working parties had been observed and places where smoke had been seen 2nd Lt J Barwell reported from M.G.C. Base and was taken on the strength of the Company from this date	

MAPS. LA BASSEE 36c NW1 Edition 8A
RICHEBOURG 36SW3 Edition 8A

Army Form C. 2118.

WAR DIARY
or
INTELLIGENCE SUMMARY

(Erase heading not required.)

202 MACHINE GUN COMPANY

Instructions regarding War Diaries and Intelligence
Summaries are contained in F. S. Regs., Part II.
and the Staff Manual respectively. Title Pages
will be prepared in manuscript.

Place	Date	Hour	Summary of Events and Information	Remarks and references to Appendices
FESTUBERT and GIVENCHY SECTORS	20.4.17	9pm to Midnight	5 guns fired indirect on enemy's back area.	
do	21.4.17	1.15pm	Our guns fired on an enemy working party – result unknown.	
do	21.4.17	9pm to Midnight	4 guns fired indirect on enemy's back area.	
do	22.4.17	10pm	In response to a call from the Officer Commanding 2/6 Bn. Lancashire Fusiliers we put a barrage on portion of the enemy's wire which had been cut, preventing him from repairing same.	
do	23.4.17	Midnight to 5AM	Gaps made in wire by our artillery were again engaged by our M.Gs.	
do	24.4.17	2.30pm to 8.30pm	Hostile artillery fired about 300 5.9 shells in the vicinity of Coy. HQ & billets at GORRE. One shell struck the billet wounding seven men, two men subsequently died of wounds.	
do	25.4.17	Midnight to 5AM	Our M.Gs. brought heavy fire to bear on gaps made in enemy's wire.	

MAPS. LA BASSEE 36C NW1 Edtn. 8A
RICHEBOURG 36 SW 3 Edtn 8A

Army Form C. 2118.

WAR DIARY
or
INTELLIGENCE SUMMARY
(Erase heading not required.)

Instructions regarding War Diaries and Intelligence Summaries are contained in F.S. Regs., Part II. and the Staff Manual respectively. Title Pages will be prepared in manuscript.

Place	Date	Hour	Summary of Events and Information	Remarks and references to Appendices
GIVENCHY and FESTUBERT SECTORS	26.4.17	Midnight to 5 AM	Usual indirect fire on enemy's communication trenches, dugouts in woods etc	
do	27.4.17	10.0pm to 11.30pm	In conjunction with our artillery & R.E. Coes T.M. & 7 guns fired indirect on enemy's communication trenches, roads and Battalion HQ	
do	28.4.17	Midnight to 6 am	Usual Indirect fire on gaps in enemy's wire	
do	29.4.17	Midnight to 5 am	Usual indirect fire on gaps in enemy's wire	
do	30.4.17	Midnight to 5 am	Usual indirect fire on gaps in enemy's wire. 12 men arrived from M.G.C. Base Depot and were taken on the strength of the Company.	
			Casualties	
			Officers men total	
			Killed or Died 11 176 187.	
			Wounded 2	
			6	
			Admitted Hospital (sick) 7	

John Robson Capt.
202nd Coy
Commanding 202nd Coy

197th Brigade.

66th Division.

202nd MACHINE GUN COMPANY MAY 1917.

WAR DIARY or INTELLIGENCE SUMMARY

Army Form C. 2118

202 Machine Gun Company

Place	Date	Hour	Summary of Events and Information	Remarks and references to Appendices
GIVENCHY and FESTUBERT SECTORS	1.5.17	8 A.M.	Strength of Company — Officers 11, Men 196, Total 187	
		8 A.M.	Our Anti-Aircraft Guns stopped Hostile Aeroplane crossing our lines	
Do	2.5.17	Do	Situation in General — Normal	
Do	3.5.17	Do	Avenue Rd Gun Position A9c 85/50 was shelled by 5.9ys Many Direct hits. Barker and McGowan Killed. The dug-out was slightly damaged	
Do	4.5.17	Do	Situation in General — Normal	
Do	5.5.17	Do	Situation in General — Normal	
Do	6.5.17	Do	Our Anti-Aircraft Guns drove back an hostile aeroplane	
Do	7.5.17	Do	Situation in General — Normal	
Do	8.5.17	Do	Lieut Langstaff wounded and was taken or Strength of Company at Sm. Admitted Hospital 6.30 P.m. (sick) Situation in General — Normal	
Do	9.5.17	Do	Situation in General — Normal	
Do	10.5.17	Do	In conjunction with the Artillery 1 machine gun carried out an organized indirect fire scheme bringing fire to bear upon the enemys Front Support Line	

Army Form C. 2118.

LA BASSEE 36cNW1 Eulus SA
RICHEBOURG 36SW3 Loker SA

WAR DIARY
or
INTELLIGENCE SUMMARY
(Erase heading not required.)

202 Machine Gun Company

Instructions regarding War Diaries and Intelligence Summaries are contained in F.S. Regs., Part II. and the Staff Manual respectively. Title Pages will be prepared in manuscript.

Place	Date	Hour	Summary of Events and Information	Remarks and references to Appendices
GIVENCHY and FESTUBERT SECTORS	11.5.17	6 AM to 8 AM	Special Brigade Orders No 1. (Extract) The Brigadier wishes to thank those Units and the men of "E" Company Special R.E. for their valuable co-operation and for the Colonel Murray and the Lefe Corps Artillery for the rapidity and effectiveness of their barrage fire, and to the NCOs then of the Light T.M. Battery and 202 M.G. Coy who also co-operated.	
Do	12.5.17	5 AM to 8 AM	Annes Rd Gun Position shelled. Emplacement completed, demolished.	
Do	13.5.17	6 AM to 8 AM	Pte Bedford wounded. Hostile Aeroplane attempted to cross our lines but was driven back by our Anti Aircraft Guns.	
Do	14.5.17	4 pm to 5 pm	7 machine guns carried out indirect overhead fire scheme engaging points on the enemy back areas. Report on preliminary examination of 2 prisoners of the 2nd Bn 1st Bav. Res. Regt. 1st Bav. Res. Div. taken in A90 on night of 13th May 1917. Extract from letter – I shall ask you pencil on monday when we are relieved, as there is always phosphate and Men Cursed machine guns on the way [illegible] get stuff forward so there is always, phosphate...

Army Form C. 2118.

WAR DIARY
or
INTELLIGENCE SUMMARY

(Erase heading not required.)

LAÅRASSE 36c NW1 Edsh. 8A
RICHEBOURG 36S/W3 Edstion 8A

1/2 Machine Gun Company

Place	Date	Hour	Summary of Events and Information	Remarks and references to Appendices
GIVENCHY and FESTUBERT SECTORS	15.5.17	8 AM to 8 AM	1 Other rank reinforcement from M.G. Base. Situation in General – Normal	
Do	16.5.17	Do	Situation in General – Normal	
Do	17.5.17	Do	Situation in General – Normal	
Do	18.5.17	Do	Reconnoitred Gun Positions with the 2nd Officer of the 1st Machine Gun Squadron Canadian Detachment. 2nd Lieut. Morrison arrived from Base and taken on strength of the company.	
Do	19.5.17	8 AM to 8 AM	Our left flank Section M.Go. relieved by a detachment of the 1st Machine Gun Squadron and the 1st Right Late Section M.Go. relieved by a detachment of the 1st M.G. Squadron.	
Do	20.5.17	Do	Company moved to LE HAMEL (X20d.) BETHONE Confused Sheet 36 A SE 36 3W Edition 6	
Do	21.5.17	8 AM to 8 AM	Company training.	
Do	22.5.17	Do	Company training. 2 O. Ranks reinforcements from Base	

Army Form C. 2118.

WAR DIARY
or
INTELLIGENCE SUMMARY
(Erase heading not required.)

LARKEE 36C NW Sht 36
FESTUBERT 36SW3 Edtn 8A

Place	Date	Hour	Summary of Events and Information	Remarks and references to Appendices
GIVENCHY and FESTUBERT SECTORS	23.5.17	8 AM to 8 PM	Company training	
do	24.5.17	do	Company training	
do	25.5.17	do	Company training	
do	26.5.17	do	We relieved the 14th M.G. Squadron and took up our former positions	
do	27.5.17	do	Left hub MG was wounded	
do	28.5.17	do	Situation in Sector Normal	
do	29.5.17	do	Hostile aeroplane attempting to cross our line was driven back by our anti aircraft guns	
do	30.5.17	do	Situation in general Normal	
do	31.5.17	do	1 Reinforcement arrived for base. Strength of Company Officers 11 Men 168 LG 179	

John Roper Capt. OC 2 in Comdng 20 MG Coy

197th Brigade.
66th Division.
9------------

202nd MACHINE GUN COMPANY JUNE 1917.

LA BASSEE 36 NW1 Edition 8A
MAPS RICHEBOURG 36 SW3 Edition 8A

Army Form C. 2118.

Instructions regarding War Diaries and Intelligence Summaries are contained in F. S. Regs., Part II. and the Staff Manual respectively. Title pages will be prepared in manuscript.

WAR DIARY
or
INTELLIGENCE SUMMARY.
(Erase heading not required.)

202nd MACHINE GUN COMPANY

Place	Date	Hour	Summary of Events and Information	Remarks and references to Appendices
GIVENCHY and FESTUBERT SECTORS	1.6.17	8.0am	Strength of Company — Officers 12, O.Ranks 168, Total 180	
		8.0am	Our guns fired indirect on enemy's communication trenches, track areas etc. Situation Normal	
do	2.6.17	do	Our Anti-Aircraft Gun prevented a hostile aeroplane crossing our lines.	
do	3.6.17	do	Situation Normal	
do	4.6.17	do	Our guns fired indirect on enemy's communication trenches, cross roads, tracks etc. 9 other ranks reinforcement arrived from Machine Gun Corps Base	
do	5.6.17	do	Machine Guns fired indirect on enemy's communication trenches, new tracks, dumps etc. Situation - Normal	
do	6.6.17	do	Gas was made on enemy's wire by the artillery was kept open by the machine guns.	
do	7.6.17	do	We fired our usual indirect programme covering important points on the enemy's back area. Roads extent transport had been heard were swept by our fire at irregular intervals. The path in the wire was kept open by material fire. Our fires. 2 other ranks wounded.	

(A7932) Wt. W12539/M1293. 752,000. 1/17. D. D. & L., Ltd. Forms/C.2118-14.

MAPS { LA BASSEE 36c NW, Sheets 8M.
       RICHEBOURCH 36 SW 3 Sheets 8A

Army Form C. 2118.

WAR DIARY
or
INTELLIGENCE SUMMARY.
(Erase heading not required.)

202nd MACHINE GUN COMPANY

Instructions regarding War Diaries and Intelligence
Summaries are contained in F. S. Regs., Part II.
and the Staff Manual respectively. Title pages
will be prepared in manuscript.

Place	Date	Hour	Summary of Events and Information	Remarks and references to Appendices
GIVENCHY and FESTUBERT SECTORS	8.6.17	8.0am to 8.0am	Machine Guns fired usual expenditure on enemy communication trenches etc. At 11.45 pm at a request from the O.C. Left Sub-Sector to fire on S.29A 00.47 – this was done immediately. 2nd Lieut F. G. Little wounded – admitted to hospital	
do	9.6.17	do	A hostile plane flying in the direction of our lines was fired at by our guns and driven back. Our special indirect fire was kept the job in the open. S. O. Ranks moved from 172nd Machine Gun Coy. Situation Normal	
do	10.6.17	do	Capt. J. Hyphen proceeded on leave to the United Kingdom Lieut. J. E. Bullock. M.C. assumed Command of the Company from this date	
do	11.6.17	do	Our machine guns co-operated in a minor operation with the 198th Infantry Brigade firing on enemy's men	
do	12.6.17	do	Communication. A hostile aeroplane attempted to cross our lines but was driven back by two machine guns	

MAPS { LA BASSEE 36c NW1 Edition 8A
       { RICHE BOURG 36 SW3 Edin 8A

Army Form C. 2118.

WAR DIARY
or
INTELLIGENCE SUMMARY.
(Erase heading not required.)

202nd MACHINE GUN COMPANY

Instructions regarding War Diaries and Intelligence Summaries are contained in F. S. Regs., Part II and the Staff Manual respectively. Title pages will be prepared in manuscript.

Place	Date	Hour	Summary of Events and Information	Remarks and references to Appendices
GIVENCHY and FESTUBERT SECTORS	13.6.17	8 p.m. to 8 a.m.	We fired our usual indirect programme on track areas and roads in enemy's area from 10 p.m. to 2.30 a.m. from 3.0 a.m. till 5 a.m. the machine guns assembled on a new operation on enemy's front system, sweeping all important communication trenches, roads, tramway tracks and Battalion Headquarters. During the operation this Gun brought heavy enfilade fire to bear upon enemy's main communication trenches. Situation Normal	
do	14.6.17	do	The Tps in enemy's wire was vas open left open.	
do	15.6.17	do		
do	16.6.17	do	Machine Guns carried out usual indirect fire on enemy's back areas. Information was received from the G.O. left Battalion that the enemy's transport could be heard on the RUE DU MARAIS. This target was engaged immediately and we reached the round after a considerable time.	

MAPS { LA BASSÉE 36c NW, Edn. 8A
       RICHEBOURG 36 S/d 3 Edn. 8A

Army Form C. 2118.

WAR DIARY
or
INTELLIGENCE SUMMARY.

(Erase heading not required.)

202nd MACHINE GUN COMPANY

Instructions regarding War Diaries and Intelligence Summaries are contained in F. S. Regs., Part II. and the Staff Manual respectively. Title pages will be prepared in manuscript.

Place	Date	Hour	Summary of Events and Information	Remarks and references to Appendices
GIVENCHY and FESTUBERT SECTORS	17.6.17	8am to 8pm	Hostile aeroplane was prevented from crossing our line by machine gun.	
do	18.6.17	do	Lieut. G. E. Gibbs M.C. attended a conference of Unit Commanders at 197th Infantry Bde Headquarters.	
do	19.6.17	do	Situation Normal. Usual harass'g fire was carried out	
do	20.6.17	do	Carried a reconnaissance of M.G. positions with the O.C. and section officers of the 6th Machine Gun Coy. The company was relieved by the 6th Machine Gun Coy.	
BELLERIVE (BETHUNE COMBINED SHEET)	21.6.17	do	G. O. Mark reinforcements arrived from Machine Gun Corps Base Camp Camiers. Company marched to BELLERIVE	
do	22.6.17	do	Re-organization and equipping of company	
do	23.6.17	do	Company training - short Route march Capt G Roberts proceeded from leave and took over Command of the company	

Army Form C. 2118.

WAR DIARY
or
INTELLIGENCE SUMMARY.

(Erase heading not required.)

202nd MACHINE GUN COMPANY

Instructions regarding War Diaries and Intelligence Summaries are contained in F. S. Regs., Part II. and the Staff Manual respectively. Title pages will be prepared in manuscript.

Place	Date	Hour	Summary of Events and Information	Remarks and references to Appendices
BETHUNE COMBINED SHEET	24.6.17	8.am	Company marched to CHOCQUES STATION. 1 O.Rank reported from hospital	
		to	Entrained for DUNKERQUE. Marched to billets at	
DUNKERQUE IA		8.pm	TETEGHEM. IGA 45.35	
Do	25.6.17	Do	Company training	
Do	26.6.17	Do	Company training	
Do	27.6.17	Do	Company training	
Do	28.6.17	Do	Company training	
Do	29.6.17	Do	Company training	
Do	30.6.17	Do	Company training. 1 O.Rank reported from hospital. 1 Rank transferred from 2/3 E. Lancs. R.A. London for duties-duties other than 10t men 197 201	

Strength of Company

Chr. Robin Craft
Comm Auchig 202 M.G.Cy

197th Brigade.
66th Division.

202nd MACHINE GUN COMPANY JULY 1917.

Confidential

War Diary
of
202nd M. G. Coy.

from July 1st 1917 to July 31st 1917

(Volume 5)

Vol 5

MAR. BELGIUM and FRANCE. VOLUME 5.
Sheet 19 Second Edition

CONFIDENTIAL

Army Form C. 2118.

WAR DIARY
or
INTELLIGENCE SUMMARY.
(Erase heading not required.)

of 2nd Bn G.Coy

Instructions regarding War Diaries and Intelligence
Summaries are contained in F. S. Regs., Part II.
and the Staff Manual respectively. Title pages
will be prepared in manuscript.

Place	Date	Hour	Summary of Events and Information	Remarks and references to Appendices
TETEGHEM	1.7.17	8am to 1pm	Strength of Company Officers 10 Men 191 Total 201	
C9A 40 40			Company training	
	2.7.17	do	Company training	
	3.7.17	do	Company training	
	4.7.17	do	Company training	
	5.7.17	do	Company training	
	6.7.17	do	Company training	
	7.7.17	do	Company training	
	8.7.17	do	Bathing Parade	
	9.7.17	do	Marched to LEFFRINCKHOUKE and took over Huts in that area. 2nd Lt. J. Whitehouse admitted to hospital (sick)	
LEFFRINCKHOUKE	10.7.17	do	Company training	
L5a 50.55	11.7.17	1am	Company Orders to "Stand By" and to move at once	
NIEUPORT BAINS	do	3.30am	Marched to JEANNINOT Camp and took over huts W18.b.5.5	
	do	10.0am	2nd Lt. E.L. Morrison admitted to hospital (sick)	
SECTOR	14.7.17	1pm	Reconnoitred and collected portions for turning over to an	
		4pm	LOMBARTZYDE SECTOR	

MAP: BELGIUM and FRANCE
Sheet 19 Second Edition
NIEUPORT 12 S.W.; Sheet No. 1A

Army Form C. 2118.

WAR DIARY
or
INTELLIGENCE SUMMARY.
(Erase heading not required.)

Instructions regarding War Diaries and Intelligence Summaries are contained in F.S. Regs., Part II. and the Staff Manual respectively. Title pages will be prepared in manuscript.

Place	Date	Hour	Summary of Events and Information	Remarks and references to Appendices
NIEUPORT BAINS SECTOR	13.7.17	1pm to 9pm	Reconnoitred and selected front positions in LOMBARTZYDE SECTOR	
	14.7.17	1.15 to 3.15	12 Gun teams with complete new equipment moved over range for positions in LOMBARTZYDE SECTOR	
Do	15.7.17	3.30	Three gun teams with 100 rpg for the enemy's artillery in attempt to retake that part of his line to LOMBARTZYDE which had been captured by us during July 10 & 11. 36,000 rounds ammunition was fired in MK companies remainder taken to TEANNINOT Camp. Gun teams with guns, gun equipment & ammunition did not get to TEANNINOT Camp.	
Do	16.9.17	2.30pm	took a section officers reconnaissance parties over C.O. and L section officers reconnaissance parties between NIEUPORT and 216 & Michie line & front between NIEUPORT & LE FEVRE Camp R.32.A. and took over	
Do	17.7.17	10AM	Company marched to LE FEVRE Camp R.32.A. and took over	
	Do	2.30pm	Relief from 216 T.M. B. Boy	
	Do	10.30pm	Company relieved 216th M.G. Coy in trenches below NIEUPORT & Sea	
NIEUPORT BAINS SECTOR	18.7.17	12.00 noon	Situation - Normal 2nd Lieut L.E. Kerr and 30 O.R L.E. Burr 7.30am also 1 O.Rank reported from M.G. Base and were taken on strength of company	

Army Form C. 2118.

WAR DIARY
or
INTELLIGENCE SUMMARY.
(Erase heading not required.)

Place	Date	Hour	Summary of Events and Information	Remarks and references to Appendices
NIEUPORT BAINS SECTOR	19.7.17	7.30am & 9am	Situation - Normal. 1.0. Route attack hoped (cancelled)	
"	20.7.17	"	Situation - Normal. 2nd Lt. M.P. Kelly wounded from M.G. Bay Dug-out was taken on the strength of the Bn.	
"	21.7.17	"	Situation - Normal	
"	22.7.17	"	Situation - Normal	
"	23.7.17	"	Situation - Normal	
"	24.7.17	"	Situation - Normal. 2 Hostile aeroplanes attempted to cross our lines and were fired upon by our machine guns	
"	25.7.17	"	Situation - Normal. 6 hostile aeroplane attempting to cross our line was fired on and driven off by our machine guns.	
"	26.7.17	"	Situation - Normal	
"	27.7.17	"	Situation - Normal	

Army Form C. 2118.

Maps NIEUPORT 1/2 SW1 Edition 1A

WAR DIARY
or
INTELLIGENCE SUMMARY

(Erase heading not required.)

Instructions regarding War Diaries and Intelligence Summaries are contained in F. S. Regs., Part II. and the Staff Manual respectively. Title Pages will be prepared in manuscript.

Place	Date	Hour	Summary of Events and Information	Remarks and references to Appendices
NIEUPORT BAINS SECTOR	28.7.17	7.30am to 7.30am	L.O. suffers of 203rd Machine Gun Coy reconnoitred position with L.O. of 202 M.G. Coy	
do	29.7.17	do	Our flank guns opened fire on pre-arranged S.O.S. lines on seeing S.O.S. put up on 49th Divisional Front. Right Section Gun position R8 & R13 relieved by 1 machine gun of 203rd M.G. Coy.	
do	30.7.17	do	Two hostile Planes were observed to fall in flames behind enemy's line. Our left Sectn Guns were relieved by 203rd M.G. Coy.	
do	31.7.17	do	Company training of Company	

Strength of Company
Officers 13
Other ranks 183
Total 196

Malcolm Hunt ?a. Captain
Commanding 202 M.G. Coy

2449 Wt. W14957/M90 750,000 1/16 J.B.C. & A. Forms/C.2118/12.

197th Brigade.
66th Division.

202nd MACHINE GUN COMPANY AUGUST 1917.

Confidential

War Diary
of
202nd Machine Gun Company

From Aug 1st 1917 to Aug 31st 1917

(Volume 6)

Army Form C. 2118.

MAP. NIEUPORT 1/10,000

WAR DIARY
or
INTELLIGENCE SUMMARY.
(Erase heading not required.)

Instructions regarding War Diaries and Intelligence
Summaries are contained in F. S. Regs., Part II.
and the Staff Manual respectively. Title pages
will be prepared in manuscript.

Place	Date	Hour	Summary of Events and Information	Remarks and references to Appendices
SURREY CAMP R 32 a	1.8.17	8 AM to 8 AM	Strength of Company Officers O.Ranks Total 13 183 196 Company Training. Capt. J.Robin proceeded on leave to the United Kingdom. Lieut. J Barker took over command of Company. Company Training.	
Do	2.8.17	Do	Company Training	
Do	3.8.17	Do	Company Training	
Do	4.8.17	Do	The 202nd M.G.Coy (less 2 sections) relieved the 199th Machine Gun Company (less 2 sections) in the COXYDE SECTOR COAST DEFENCE at 8 AM. Remaining half company on Company Training. Three Runners	
Do	5.8.17	Do	The 202nd Machine Gun Company in COXYDE SECTOR COAST DEFENCE (less officers and NCOs were relieved by 148th Machine Gun Company (less officers and NCOs))	

Army Form C. 2118.

WAR DIARY
or
INTELLIGENCE SUMMARY.
(Erase heading not required.)

Instructions regarding War Diaries and Intelligence Summaries are contained in F. S. Regs., Part II. and the Staff Manual respectively. Title pages will be prepared in manuscript.

MAP NIEUPORT 1/10,000

Place	Date	Hour	Summary of Events and Information	Remarks and references to Appendices
SURREY CAMP R32A	5.8.17	8AM to 8AM	Continued. Special Barrage Positions commenced at M21C.	
Do	6.8.17	Do	Company Training. Construction of Barrage Positions at M21C continued. 2nd Lt. J. Barrett admitted hospital (sick)	
Do	7.8.17	Do	Company Training	
Do	8.8.17	Do	Company Training	
Do	9.8.17	Do	Company Training. Officers & NCOs of 202nd M.G. Coy in the CONDE SECTOR COAST DEFENCE. Officer Commanding 202nd and Officer commanding 204th M.G. Coy reconnoitred Harassing Fire Positions at M26B	
Do	10.8.17	Do	202nd M.G. Coy relieved 204th M.G. Coy in Harassing Fire Positions at M26B. Commenced harassing fire on enemy's back areas. Communication trenches - Company Training	

Remarks.

Army Form C. 2118.

WAR DIARY
or
INTELLIGENCE SUMMARY.
(Erase heading not required.)

MAP NIEUPORT 1/10,000

Instructions regarding War Diaries and Intelligence Summaries are contained in F. S. Regs., Part II. and the Staff Manual respectively. Title pages will be prepared in manuscript.

Place	Date	Hour	Summary of Events and Information	Remarks and references to Appendices
SURREY CAMP	11.8.17	8AM to 8AM	Company having O.C. & Divisional Machine Gun Officer reconnoitred Hindenburg line positions at M26B. One horse teams of Co. wounded, and 1 other wounded by shell fire during reconnaissance. Having fire continued according to programme laid down by Divisional Machine Gun Officer.	
Do	12.8.17	Do	Church Parade	
Do	13.8.17	Do	Extra section Rifles of Hindenburg line positions. Harassing fire continued.	
Do	14.8.17	Do	Company training. Harassing fire continues.	
Do	15.8.17	Do	Company training. The remaining section of 202nd M.G.Coy. proceeded to especially prepared positions at M24C to carry out barrage organisation in conjunction with operations carried out by Special Company R.E.'s. Half Company returned to Company HQ on completion of operations	

(A7092). Wt. W12859/M1293. 75,000. 1/17. D.D. & L., Ltd. Forms/C2118/14.

Army Form C. 2118.

MAP. NIEUPORT 1/10,000

WAR DIARY
or
INTELLIGENCE SUMMARY.
(Erase heading not required.)

Instructions regarding War Diaries and Intelligence Summaries are contained in F. S. Regs., Part II. and the Staff Manual respectively. Title pages will be prepared in manuscript.

Place	Date	Hour	Summary of Events and Information	Remarks and references to Appendices
SURREY CAMP R32a	16.8.17	8 AM to 8 AM	Company Training. Capt J Roton returned from leave	
Do	17.8.17	to	Company Training. Capt Roton took over duties of Divisional Machine Gun Officer. 66th Division 202nd M G Coy was relieved by 203rd M G Coy in harassing fire positions	
Do	18.8.17	to	Company Training.	
Do	19.8.17	to	Company Training. O.C. reconnoitred positions with O.C. 202 M.G.Coy in NIEUPORT BAINS SECTOR	
NIEUPORT BAINS SECTOR	20.8.17	to	202nd M.G.Coy relieved 201 M.G.Coy in RIGHT SECTOR	
	21.8.17	to	202nd M.G.Coy relieved 204 M.G.Coy in LEFT SECTOR	
NIEUPORT BAINS				

Army Form C. 2118.

WAR DIARY
or
INTELLIGENCE SUMMARY.

(Erase heading not required.)

MAP. NIEUPORT 1/10,000

Instructions regarding War Diaries and Intelligence Summaries are contained in F. S. Regs., Part II. and the Staff Manual respectively. Title pages will be prepared in manuscript.

Place	Date	Hour	Summary of Events and Information	Remarks and references to Appendices
NIEUPORT BAINS SECTOR	22.8.17	8AM	Situation Normal.	
		8AM	OC attended conference at Corps HQ	
Do	23.8.17	Do	Enemy Aeroplane prevented from crossing our lines afterwards damaged by our Machine Gun fire. Situation Normal	
Do	24.8.17	Do	Situation Normal. M.E. Emplacement reported at M15d.3+	
Do	25.8.17	Do	One of our machine guns fired direct on BOG AVENUE M15a.9.3. Lieut. G.E. Elkins MC retired from M.G. Corps Reinforcements and took over Command of Company.	
Do	26.8.17	Do	Situation Normal. CRE and Corps Machine Gun officer Reconnoitred fresh selected New Position for Gun Scheme of defence for	NIEUPORT BAINS AREA
Do	27.8.17	Do	Situation Normal. + other reconnoitred shell fire	

Army Form C. 2118.

MAP: NIEUPORT 1/10000

WAR DIARY
or
INTELLIGENCE SUMMARY
(Erase heading not required.)

Instructions regarding War Diaries and Intelligence Summaries are contained in F. S. Regs., Part II. and the Staff Manual respectively. Title pages will be prepared in manuscript.

Place	Date	Hour	Summary of Events and Information	Remarks and references to Appendices
NIEUPORT BAINS SECTOR	28.8.17	8 AM to 8 AM	Situation Normal	
Do	29.8.17	Do	Situation Normal	
Do	30.8.17	Do	Lieut. J. Banks proceeded on a Machine Gun Course at CAMIERS.	
Do	31.8.17	Do	Situation Normal. An hostile aeroplane attempting to cross our lines was fired upon by our machine guns. Strength of Company. Officers 10, Ranks 172. Total 182	

C.E. Gilbert Lieut.
Commanding 202 M.G. Co.

197th Brigade.

66th Division.

202nd MACHINE GUN COMPANY SEPTWMBER 1917.

ORIGINAL

C O N F I D E N T I A L.

W A R   D I A R Y

of

202   MACHINE GUN COMPANY.

From :- 1st. September 1917.   To:- 30th. September 1917.

(V O L U M E   8).

****

Army Form C. 2118.

WAR DIARY
or
INTELLIGENCE SUMMARY

(Erase heading not required.)

MAP. Sheet 11 S.E. 1/20,000
12.S.W. 1/20,000
5 1/10,000

Instructions regarding War Diaries and Intelligence Summaries are contained in F. S. Regs., Part II. and the Staff Manual respectively. Title Pages will be prepared in manuscript.

Place	Date	Hour	Summary of Events and Information	Remarks and references to Appendices
NIEUPORT BAINS SECTOR	1.9.17	8 a.m. 8 a.m.	Strength of Company - Officers 10 Other Ranks 172 Total 182 Situation normal.	
Do.	2.9.17	Do.	Our guns prevented an hostile aeroplane from crossing over our lines. Situation normal	
Do.	3.9.17	Do.	2 Sections of 202nd M.G. Coy. were relieved by 2 Sections of 203rd M.G. Coy in Maurice A. Right Sub-Sector. (Relief Orders attached).	
Do.	4.9.17	Do.	The remaining 2 Sections were relieved by the remaining Sections of 203rd M.G.Cy in Left Sub-Sector. (Relief Orders attached.)	
SURREY CAMP R. 32 A.	5.9.17	Do.	Company training	
Do.	6.9.17	Do.	Company training	
Do.	7.9.17	Do.	Company training. 2nd Lt. Emmett rejoined from M.G. Base, and was taken on strength of Company	
Do.	8.9.17	Do.	Company training	

Army Form C. 2118.

WAR DIARY
or
INTELLIGENCE SUMMARY.
(Erase heading not required.)

Instructions regarding War Diaries and Intelligence Summaries are contained in F.S. Regs., Part II. and the Staff Manual respectively. Title pages will be prepared in manuscript.

Place	Date	Hour	Summary of Events and Information	Remarks and references to Appendices
SURREY CAMP R 3D A	9.9.17	8 AM to 8 AM	Church Parade. - Enemy shelled billet rather heavily during the night. Lieut. J. E. Kerr and 2nd Lieut. Hedley reported from M.G. Base, and one taken on strength of Company.	
Do	10.9.17	Do	Company Training - 2nd Lieut. Hedley reported from M.G. Base, and was taken on strength of Company.	
Do	11.9.17	Do	Company Training	
Do	12.9.17	Do	Company Training	
Do	13.9.17	Do	Company Training	
NIEUPORT BAINS SECTOR	14.9.17	Do	Company Training. 204 M.G. Coy. were relieved by 6 gun teams of 202 M.G. Coy. in Harassing Fire Positions. Two Working Parties were attached to the R.E.s who were making M.G. Emplacements, and Dugouts, etc.	
Do	15.9.17	Do	Heavy harassing fire was brought to bear on the enemy's back areas.	

Army Form C. 2118.

WAR DIARY
or
INTELLIGENCE SUMMARY
(Erase heading not required.)

Instructions regarding War Diaries and Intelligence Summaries are contained in F. S. Regs., Part II. and the Staff Manual respectively. Title Pages will be prepared in manuscript.

Place	Date	Hour	Summary of Events and Information	Remarks and references to Appendices
NIEUPORT BAINS SECTOR	15.9.17		Communications, etc.,	
Do.	16.9.17	8 AM to 8 AM	Enemy's back areas and roads were again fired on by our harassing fire guns throughout the night.	
Do.	17.9.17	Do.	Harassing fire continued according to programme laid down by D.R.G.O. 88th Division.	
Do.	18.9.17	Do.	Our harassing fire guns paid special attention to new work under construction by the enemy in back areas.	
Do.	19.9.17	Do.	No harassing fire done owing to infantry relief.	
Do.	20.9.17	Do.	Harassing fire continued in accordance with programme received from D.R.G.O. 66th Division.	
Do.	21.9.17	Do.	Harassing fire continued	
Do.	22.9.17	Do.	Do.	
Do.	23.9.17	Do.	Gun teams in harassing fire position and working parties withdrawn to Bde. H.Q.	

MAPS. BELGIUM & FRANCE. Sheet 12. 1/40,000
BELGIUM & PART of FRANCE 1/40,000 Sheet 27

Army Form C. 2118.

WAR DIARY
or
INTELLIGENCE SUMMARY.
(Erase heading not required.)

Instructions regarding War Diaries and Intelligence Summaries are contained in F. S. Regs., Part II. and the Staff Manual respectively. Title pages will be prepared in manuscript.

Place	Date	Hour	Summary of Events and Information	Remarks and references to Appendices
BRAY DUNES	24-9-17	8 AM to 8 AM	Company marched to BRAY DUNES DQ 2. and took over Coast defences from 97th Infty Bde., at ZUYDCOOTE C4C for one night.	
D°	25.9.17	D°	Company training.	
ARQUES	26.9.17	D°	2 Other Ranks wounded in Air Raid. The 202 M.G. Coy Transport Section proceeded to ARQUES by road.	
D°	27.9.17	D°	The remainder of the Company proceeded to ARQUES S 15 (Sheet 27) by train & lorry.	
D°	28.9.17	D°	Lieut. Barber rejoined Company from M.G. Corps Canniers, and assumed duties of 2nd in Command of the Company	
D°	29.9.17	D°	Lieut Paulson proceeded to FLIXECOURT on 4th Army Infantry Course. 202nd M.G. Coy took part in Brigade Manoeuvres	
D°	30.9.17	D°	The 202nd M.G. Coy, again took part in Batt. training (Attack & Counter attack work).	

Strength of Company
Officers 10
Other Ranks 176
Total 186

G.E. Gilbert Captain,
Commanding 202 M.G. Company

202nd M.G. Coy

Operation Order No 30 A/

Map Ref.

    Sheet 11 SE   1/20,000
    Sheet 12 SW   1/20,000
    Sheet No 5   1/10,000

1. The 202nd Machine Gun Coy will be relieved in the NIEUPORT BAINS SECTOR by 203rd M.G. Coy on the 3rd & 4th September 1917.

2. RIGHT SUB SECTOR at 9.30pm 3.9.17
(See appendix "A")
LEFT SUB-SECTOR at 9.30pm 4.9.17
(See appendix "B")

3. All air photos, defence scheme, trench stores and such maps as were taken over from 204th Machine Gun Coy will be handed over and receipts forwarded to Coy HQ by 5AM on the day following relief.

4. All guns, tripods, belt boxes and

gun equipment etc will be brought out and packed in limbers (See Appendices "A" & "B")

5. Section Officers will remain with the in-coming sections until their reliefs are thoroughly conversant with the scheme of defence and positions of the guns.

6. The relieving sections on being relieved will march to SURREY CAMP R32A

7. <u>Transport</u>
O.C Transport will make the necessary arrangements for conveying Guns & gun equipment to Coy HQ

8. Completion of relief will be reported to this office using code word "HERBERT"

9. Acknowledge

G.E. Gibbert
Lieut
Comdg 20th M.G Coy

3·9·1917

Copies to:-

	No 1	DMGO
	„ 2	OC 203 MG Coy
	„ 3	OC No 1 Section
	„ 4	„ No 2 „
	„ 5	„ No 3 „
	„ 6	„ No 4 „
	„ 7	Transport Officer
	„ 8	War Diary
	„ 9	„ „
	„ 10	File

Appendix "A"

RIGHT SUB-SECTOR

1. Nos 1 & 2 Sections will be relieved by 2 Sections of the 203rd M.G. Coy at 9.30pm 3.9.1917

2. One guide from each Section will be sent to the LAITERIE ROYALE by 9.30pm to guide relieving sections to section HQ via ROUTE EOLIENNE

3. One guide per gun team will be at SECTION HQ at 10pm to guide gun teams to their respective positions

4. 1 NCO & 10 men per section will report at SECTION HQ at 10pm to act as carrying party

5. <u>Transport</u>
   2 limbers will be at the RATION DUMP at 11pm to take guns & gun equipment etc to Coy HQ

3.9.1917   Lieut
                 Comdg 202 M.G. Coy

Appendix "B"

LEFT SUB SECTOR & HQ

1. Nos 3 & 4 Sections & HQ. will be relieved by 2 Sections & HQ of 203rd M.G. Coy @ 9.30pm 4.9.17

2. One guide per section will be at LAITERIE ROYALE at 9.20pm to guide relieving sections to Section HQ

3. One guide per gun team will be at Section HQ at 10pm to guide gun teams to their respective positions

4. 1 NCO & 10 men per section will report at SECTION HQ at 10pm to act as carrying party.

5. <u>Transport</u>.
   2 Limbers will be at LAITERIE ROYALE at 11pm to take back guns & gun equipment etc to Coy HQ
   1 Limber will be at LAITERIE ROYALE at 8pm to take back to Coy HQ HQ material

G.E. Gilbert Lieut
Comdg 20 M.G. Coy

3.9.1917

197th Brigade.

66th Division.

202nd MACHINE GUN COMPANY OCTOBER 1917.

CONFIDENTIAL

War Diary
of
202nd M G Coy

From 1.10.1917 — 31.10.1917

(Volume 8)

Army Form C. 2118.

Map. Ref. Sheet 27 1/40.000

WAR DIARY
or
INTELLIGENCE SUMMARY
(Erase heading not required.)

Instructions regarding War Diaries and Intelligence Summaries are contained in F. S. Regs., Part II. and the Staff Manual respectively. Title Pages will be prepared in manuscript.

Place	Date	Hour	Summary of Events and Information	Remarks and references to Appendices
ARQUES S.1/3O 70.80	1.10.17	8 AM to 8 AM	Strength of Company Officers 10 Ranks 176 Total 176 Company training	
EECKE area	2.10.17	Do	The company moved to EECKE area and took over billets at Q 20 d 85 70.	
Do	3.10.17	Do	Company training	
Do	4.10.17	Do	2nd/Lt. Kelley P. and 22 Ranks were dispatched to Corps Reinforcement Camp MORBECQ. The company marched to WINNEZEELE and took over billets at F 9 a 1.8	
WINNEZEELE AREA	5.10.17	Do	The Company entrained with 199th Inf. Bde. to VLAMERTINGHE. Company detrained and marched to YPRES. At 10 pm the company proceeded to the trenches and relieved the 9th, 11th & 23rd Australian Machine Gun Companies in the BARRAGE line position	

2449 Wt. W14957/M90 750,000 1/16 J.B.C. & A. Forms/C.2118/12.

ZONNE BEKE 21 NEI
8.a.7a
1/10/170

Army Form C. 2118.

WAR DIARY
or
INTELLIGENCE SUMMARY
(Erase heading not required.)

Place	Date	Hour	Summary of Events and Information	Remarks and references to Appendices
ZONNE BEKE SECTOR	6.10.17	8AM to 9AM	At 7pm the S.O.S. was put up on the Divisional Front. Our machine guns fired on S.O.S. barrage lines	
do	7.10.17	do	At 4.30am the S.O.S. was put up on the Divisional Front. Our machine guns fired protective barrage on S.O.S. lines	
do	8.10.17	do	Conference of Ind. commanders at Brigade H.Q. Attack to take place on 9th Oct 1917. General scheme of attack outlined by the Brigadier	
do	9.10.17	do 3pm 4pm	Operations orders issued to Section Officers. (See attached O.O. No.31) the company was withdrawn from Barrage line positions Section officers of Nos 2 & 4 Sections reconnoitred front line to establish forward dumps of S.A.A Section Officers of Nos 1 & 3 Sections under Lieut. Barke acting under direct orders of the Divisional Machine Gun Officer went forward to select and prepare Barrage positions	

Army Form C. 2118.

WAR DIARY
or
INTELLIGENCE SUMMARY
(Erase heading not required.)

Instructions regarding War Diaries and Intelligence Summaries are contained in F. S. Regs, Part II. and the Staff Manual respectively. Title Pages will be prepared in manuscript.

Place	Date	Hour	Summary of Events and Information	Remarks and references to Appendices
ZONNEBEKE J.7.A 1/10,000 SECTOR	8/10/17	7pm	Nos 2 & 4 Sections went forward to position of assembly. HQ. Company	
do		8pm	moved forward to position of assembly.	
do	9/10/17	1am	2 & 4 Sections took up positions at point of assembly with guns, ammunition etc declining enemies's heavy fire, casualties in moving up. The gun teams being too depleted it was found impracticable to send 8 guns forward with the attack, owing to the fact that we had not sufficient men to bring up ammunition. The Commanding Officer therefore decided to send 5 guns forward with the 35th Bn. Inf. to assist in an attack on the "Red Line", and 2 guns under covering section of the	

ZONNEBEKE J NE1 J 7A 1/10,000

WAR DIARY or INTELLIGENCE SUMMARY

Army Form C. 2118.

Place: ZONNEBEKE SHEET 28 NE1
Sq 7A 1/10,000

Place	Date	Hour	Summary of Events and Information	Remarks and references to Appendices
ZONNEBEKE SECTOR	9.10.17		Lieut. Dacken with 2/6 Lewis guns to take up position in the BLUE LINE and to be prepared to repel any counter-attack made on the RIGHT FLANK of the Brigade.	
do		5.20am	Our Artillery Barrage opened, accurately. Infantry not yet arrived.	
do		5.50am	First company of 2/6 Lancs Fus arrived and proceeded to attack the RED LINE. 2/8 L.F. Coys with 3 guns followed by 2/8 Lancs Fus and 2/5 Lancs Fus arrived and pushed on with the attack. Lt. Dacken and 2 guns went forward.	
do		6.20am	2/Lt. A.E. Cross wounded	
do		7.0am		
do		10.0am	A message received from Lt. Dacken to the effect that the attack on the BLUE LINE, with guns, were put out of action, and members of the	

2449 Wt. W14957/M90 750,000 1/16 J.B.C. & A. Forms/C.2118/12.

WAR DIARY or INTELLIGENCE SUMMARY

Army Form C. 2118.

Place: ZONNEBEKE SECTOR
Date/Hour: ZONNEBEKE ZONE I / U7A / 1/19,000

Place	Date	Hour	Summary of Events and Information	Remarks and references to Appendices
ZONNEBEKE SECTOR	9.10.17	10am	Guns teams with the exception of 1 man have become casualties.	
		10.30am	2nd Lt Emmett was sent up to take command of 3 guns vice 2nd Lt Enos, with instructions to push on to avant in repelling counter-attack after the BLUE LINE had been captured and consolidated.	
		10.45a	Report was received from 2nd Lt. Howard (Intelligence Offr) 2/9th Lancs Fus. that the LEFT FLANK of 197th Infantry Brigade was being enfiladed by machine gun and rifle fire and that communication had not been established by the 2/6th Lancs Fus. on the LEFT.	

Army Form C. 2118.

WAR DIARY
or
INTELLIGENCE SUMMARY

(Erase heading not required.)

Instructions regarding War Diaries and Intelligence Summaries are contained in F. S. Regs, Part II. and the Staff Manual respectively. Title Pages will be prepared in manuscript.

Place	Date	Hour	Summary of Events and Information	Remarks and references to Appendices
ZONNEBEKE SECTOR	9.10.17	10.45am	A message was received from Lieut Barker to the effect that the Barrage Guns were not in action owing to the fact that it was impossible to bring sufficient ammunition up. The Company Commander therefore decided to use the barrage guns to replace the No 2 attacking guns that have been knocked out.	
		11.am	2nd/Lt. Beckwith with 3 guns was sent to take up position providing LEFT FLANK of the 197th Bde. 2nd/Lt Tunnell wounded. Cpl J. Wilds took over command of the 3 guns of No 2 Section, and pushed on to a position about 200 yards in front of RED LINE.	
		4 pm	Infantry were compelled to withdraw and take up position on RED LINE.	

ZONNEBEKE ZONE 1
Lu 7A
M.O. 000

Army Form C. 2118.

N.f. R.f. Div. 27 1/45,000
ZONNEBEKE 28 NE1

WAR DIARY
or
INTELLIGENCE SUMMARY

(Erase heading not required.)

Instructions regarding War Diaries and Intelligence Summaries are contained in F. S. Regs., Part II. and the Staff Manual respectively. Title Pages will be prepared in manuscript.

Place	Date	Hour	Summary of Events and Information	Remarks and references to Appendices
ZONNEBEKE SECTOR	9.10.17	5:30pm	Enemy counter-attacked and were reported to have recaptured RED LINE.	
		5:45pm	3 guns were placed in our original support line to prevent the enemy from breaking through.	
		6.0pm	2/Rifl. Bickerdike reported that his 2 guns had been put out of action and his Gun teams had sustained heavy casualties. All two Guns and reinforcements were sent up with instructions that they should be placed on the flanks of the original Brigade front so as to stand before the attack.	
do	10.10.17	5am	It was reported that the Brigade were holding a line approximately 100 yards S. WEST of RED LINE. That no communication had been established with the 2/6th Lanc. Fus. or the 195th Inf. Bde on the LEFT.	

Army Form C. 2118.

WAR DIARY
or
INTELLIGENCE SUMMARY

(Erase heading not required.)

Instructions regarding War Diaries and Intelligence Summaries are contained in F. S. Regs., Part II. and the Staff Manual respectively. Title Pages will be prepared in manuscript.

Place	Date	Hour	Summary of Events and Information	Remarks and references to Appendices
ZONNE BEKE SECTOR	10/10/17	8am	2/Lt. Bickerstaffe with 2 guns was ordered to take up positions on the LEFT FLANK of the Brigade	
		8am	2/Lt. Selly with 4 guns was ordered to take up position in our original front line	
		1pm	2/Lt. Lilly reported that 1 gun had been put out of action	
		3pm	One gun at Company Hd Qrs. out of action	
"	11/10/17	3am	A message was received from Cpl. F. White (through Brigade Hd) that his 3 guns were in position about 200 yards in front of RED LINE and that all his ammunition had been exhausted. Instructions were sent to Cpl. White to withdraw	
		8am	guns and report to Coy Hd.	
		Dawn	The Company was relieved by the 11th Australian	

Army Form C. 2118.

WAR DIARY
or
INTELLIGENCE SUMMARY
(Erase heading not required.)

Place	Date	Hour	Summary of Events and Information	Remarks and references to Appendices
ZONNEBEKE SECTOR	11.10.17		Machine Gun Company the Company marched to the asylum YPRES where they entrained for WINNEZEELE and took over billets at Iquel I.8.	
WINNEZEELE AREA	12.10.17	8 AM to 9 AM	Checking of Lewis Equipment etc. Casualties from 1st Oct to 11th Oct	
do	13.10.17	do	Re-organization 2 Off Rielly and 22 ORanks returned from Reinforcement Camp	
do	14.10.17	do	Re-organization	
do	15.10.17	do	do	
do	16.10.17	do	do	
do	17.10.17	do	do	

Army Form C. 2118.

WAR DIARY
or
INTELLIGENCE SUMMARY

(Erase heading not required.)

Map Ref Sheet 27 1/40,000

Place	Date	Hour	Summary of Events and Information	Remarks and references to Appendices
WINNEZEELE Area	18.10.17	8 AM to 9 AM	Company training. 2nd Lt. N. E. Heaven and 2nd Lt. J. Huddleston and 11 O. Ranks reported from M. E. Base and were taken on the strength of the company.	
do	19.10.17	do	Company training	
do	20.10.17	do	The company marched to RENESCURE AREA and took over billets at T 26 A 75.75	
RENESCURE AREA	21.10.17	AD	Church Parade	
do	22.10.17	do	Company training	
do	23.10.17	do	Company training	
do	24.10.17	do	Company training	
do	25.10.17	do	Company training	

Map Ref Sheet 27 1/40,000

WAR DIARY
or
INTELLIGENCE SUMMARY
(Erase heading not required.)

Army Form C. 2118.

Place	Date	Hour	Summary of Events and Information	Remarks and references to Appendices
RENESCURE AREA	25.10.17	7AM to 8AM	The following NCOs. men of the company were awarded the Military Medal :— 65809 2/Cpl W.H. Borat 60980 " H.H. Broad 65683 Pte F.C.H. Ellis 65764 " H. Hopkin 63347 " W.E. Heard 27598 " J. Taylor	
do	26.10.17		Company Training	
do	27.10.17		Company Training. The following decorations were awarded the Company:— 2/Lt. J.J. Bickerstaffe — Military Cross 67691 Cpl. J. White — Distinguished Conduct Medal 72501 Pte. E. Taylor — Military Medal	

War Diary — Army Form C. 2118

Place	Date	Hour	Summary of Events and Information	Remarks and references to Appendices
RENESCURE AREA	28.10.17	9 AM to 9 AM	Repacking Limbers.	
do	29.10.17	do	The Division was inspected by the Commander-in-Chief Sir Douglas Haig. K.T., G.C.B., G.C.V.O., K.C.I.E.	
do	30.10.17	do	Company training. 2/Lt W.E. Whitton reported from M.E. Base and was taken on the strength of the Company. The Company took part in a Brigade tactical scheme.	
do	31.10.17	do	Presentation of Medal Ribbons by Lt General the Hon. Sir H.A. Lawrence K.C.B. Commander Major General. Strength of Company Officers 10 O.Ranks 175 Total 185	

L. 11.1917

G.E. Ebert Captain
Commanding 202 M.G. Coy

Operation Order No 37

Captain G E Gilbert M.C.
Commanding 202 M.G. Coy

In the Field
8.10.1917

Map Ref PASSCHENDAELE (Parts of Sheets 20 & 28)

General Idea. The 197th Infantry Brigade has been ordered to attack and capture the objectives RED & BLUE LINES on Oct 9th 1917

Action of ~~Special Idea~~ Infantry The 3/5 Lancs Fus will attack and capture the first objective RED LINE approximately from D11c 65.30 to D17B 55.33 at Zero. At zero plus 106 the 2/6th and 2/8th Lancs Fus will pass through the RED LINE and attack the BLUE LINE approx D12A 30.25 to D18A 10.00 The 2/7 Lancs Fus will be in reserve.

Machine gun cooperation The 202nd M.G. Coy has been ordered to assist the attack. Guns will be allotted as follows:-

8 guns to go forward with the attacking infantry and assist in the consolidation

8 guns under Lieut Garber acting under the direct orders of the D.M.G.O will be used for Barrage supporting fire during the attack, and will be prepared to provide a protective

barrage beyond the final objective when it has been captured by the Infantry.

Instructions No 2 Section (4 guns) under the command of 2/Lieut Cross will move behind the 3/5 Lanc Fus, and when the RED LINE has been captured and consolidated and will take up positions to repel counter-attacks, and if the opportunity occurs to fire on the retreating enemy.

No 4 Section (4 guns) under the command of Lieut Dalton will move behind the 2/6th & 2/8th Lancr Fus. and when the BLUE LINE has been captured, will move up to assist in the consolidation. Two of these guns will be specially detailed to take up positions on the RIGHT FLANK of the Brigade. The fire of these guns should be directed towards the front of the Australian Brigade on our RIGHT, as the counter attack is expected from that direction. Special attention should be paid to the RAILWAY EMBANKMENT and VIENNA COTTAGE

Nos 2 & 4 Section will be withdrawn from the present Barrage Positions at 3 am on 8.10.1917

Lt Dalton and 2nd Lt Cross will go forward to our present support line and select positions to establish forward dumps of belt boxes + SAA

Equipment
The following equipment will be taken forward in the initial stage of the attack:-
8 Belt Boxes Ammn per gun team
1 Petrol Can of Water
1st Aid Case
Condenser Bag Tube
2 days rations will be taken
The remainder of 6 belt boxes per gun team and 2000 rounds SAA per team will be placed in the forward dump. These will be moved forward as the attack progresses
6 of the attached men will be allotted per section for carrying ammunition up to gun teams

Point of Assembly
Nos 2 & 4 Sections will should be in their position behind the tape line by 2 am on the 9.10.17

Pack Mules
4 Pack Mules per section will

report to Ration Dump at 4pm on 8.10.17. Guides will be sent to conduct them to the present barrage position

H.Q. Company H.Q. will move to Point of Assembly at 8pm on 8.10.17 and will be located at approx. D.16.d.70.65 (near the railway)

Zero. Zero hour will be notified later.

G.E. Elliot. Captain
Commanding 20th M.G. Coy.

Copies to:- 1. No 2 Section
2.   4
3.   Lt Barker
4.   War Diary
5.   "   "
6.   File.

197th Brigade.

66th Division.

202nd MACHINE GUN COMPANY NOVEMBER 1917.

CONFIDENTIAL

War Diary
of
202 Machine Gun Coy

From 1.11.1917   To 30.11.17

Volume 9.

Army Form C. 2118.

M.G. Ref. BELGIUM v FRANCE
Sheets 27 & 28.

WAR DIARY
or
INTELLIGENCE SUMMARY.
(Erase heading not required.)

Instructions regarding War Diaries and Intelligence Summaries are contained in F.S. Regs., Part II. and the Staff Manual respectively. Title pages will be prepared in manuscript.

Place	Date	Hour	Summary of Events and Information	Remarks and references to Appendices
RENESCURE AREA	1.11.17	8 AM to 8 AM	Strength of Company Officers 10 O.Ranks 175 Total 185	
do	2.11.17	do	Company training	
do	3.11.17	do	Company training	
do	4.11.17	do	Company training	
do	5.11.17	do	Church Parade	
do	5.11.17	do	Inspection of Company Transport by Brigadier General Commanding 197th Infantry Brigade	
do	6.11.17	do	The company co-operated in a Brigade Tactical Scheme	
do	7.11.17	do	Company training and packing limbers	
WEST OUTRE AREA	8.11.17	do	Entrained to WEST = OUTRE.	
YPRES	9.11.17	do	Marched to Infantry Barracks YPRES	
YPRES SECTOR			Relieved 8 machine guns of the 1st Australian Machine Gun Coy in the front line of the ZONNEBEKE SECTOR.	
ZONNEBEKE SECTOR			During the relief 2 men were killed and 2 men wounded.	

Army Form C. 2118.

WAR DIARY
or
INTELLIGENCE SUMMARY.

(Erase heading not required.)

Maps Ref: BELGIUM & FRANCE
Sheets 27, 28

Instructions regarding War Diaries and Intelligence Summaries are contained in F.S. Regs., Part II. and the Staff Manual respectively. Title pages will be prepared in manuscript.

Place	Date	Hour	Summary of Events and Information	Remarks and references to Appendices
ZONNEBEKE SECTOR	10.11.17	8 AM to 8 AM	Improved gun positions in the line.	
do	11.11.17	do	Alternate emplacements selected and work commenced. Inter-section relief.	
do	12.11.17	do	Work continued on emplacements.	
do	13.11.17	do	On the S.O.S. being put on our front, all the guns teams "STOOD TO". The enemy attempted a direct hit on one of the dug-outs killing 2 men and wounding 2 of the gun teams. The gun gear was completely destroyed.	
do	14.11.17	do	Inter-section relief. Position improved.	
do	15.11.17	do	Trench routine work and improvements made to emplacements.	
do	16.11.17	do	One elevating gear of tripod destroyed by shell fire.	

Army Form C. 2113.

Map Ref. BELGIUM & FRANCE Sheet 27 o 28

WAR DIARY
or
INTELLIGENCE SUMMARY.
(Erase heading not required.)

Place	Date	Hour	Summary of Events and Information	Remarks and references to Appendices
ZONNEBEKE SECTOR	17.11.17	8 AM to 8 AM	Inter-Section Relief.	
do	18.11.17	do	Continued improving position. Like Company relieved 203 M.G Cy relieved the 8 M. guns of this company in the front-line. This company relieved the 8 machine guns of 203 M.G.Cy in the BARRAGE POSITION.	
do	19.11.17	do	Our guns opened fire on the SOS heavy barrage on our front.	
do	20.11.17	do	Our guns fired on several enemy aeroplanes which attempted to cross our lines.	
do	21.11.17	do	On the "SOS" being put up our guns opened fire. Arranged SOS lines immediately fire arranged.	
do	22.11.17	do	Our anti-aircraft guns opened fire several times during the day and enemy aircraft. Batt. O.C. E.W.J. proceeded on leave to U.K. Lieut W.H. Keenan took over Command of Company	

Army Form C. 2118.

Maps: Sheets 27 & 28 BELGIUM and WAR DIARY
FRANCE   or
INTELLIGENCE SUMMARY.

Instructions regarding War Diaries and Intelligence
Summaries are contained in F. S. Regs., Part II.
and the Staff Manual respectively. Title pages
will be prepared in manuscript.

(Erase heading not required.)

Place	Date	Hour	Summary of Events and Information	Remarks and references to Appendices
ZONNEBEKE SECTOR	23/11/17	8AM to 8AM	This Company was relieved by the 146th M. G. Coy and on completion of relief marched to the transport	
do	24/11/17	do	lines at CAFÉ BELGE. Inspection of arms &c.	
BERTHEN AREA	25/11/17	do	Marched to BERTHEN AREA.	
STAPLE AREA	26/11/17	do	Entrained to STAPLE AREA and took over billets at U18.b.1.2.	
do	27/11/17	do	Checking Gun Equipment	
do	28/11/17	do	Baths	
do	29/11/17	do	Company training	
do	30/11/17	do	Company training. Strength of Company Officers 10, Other Ranks 164, Total 174	

M.H. Kerry ? Capt
Comdy 202 M. G. Coy

197th Brigade.

66th Division.

202nd MACHINE GUN COMPANY DECEMBER 1917.

CONFIDENTIAL

WAR DIARY

of

202ⁿᵈ MACHINE GUN COMPANY

FROM 1.12.17   TO 31.12.17

Volume 10.

CONFIDENTIAL

Map Ref. BELGIUM & FRANCE Sheet 27

Army Form C. 2118.

WAR DIARY
or
INTELLIGENCE SUMMARY.

(Erase heading not required.)

Instructions regarding War Diaries and Intelligence Summaries are contained in F. S. Regs., Part II. and the Staff Manual respectively. Title pages will be prepared in manuscript.

Place	Date	Hour	Summary of Events and Information	Remarks and references to Appendices
STAPLE AREA	1.12.17	8am to 9am	Strength of Company Officers Other ranks Total 10 164 174 Company Training Conference at Brigade HQ of Commanding Officers	
do	2.12.17	do	Church Parade	
do	3.12.17	do	Route March	
do	4.12.17	do	Company Training	
do	5.12.17	do	Bath Parade. 18 other ranks reinforcements reported for in & Base	
do	6.12.17	do	Company Training	
do	7.12.17	do	Route March. Lieut. R Dobson proceeded on leave to U.K. Conference at Brigade HQ of Commanding Officers	
do	8.12.17	do	Company Training and Lewis Practice on Range Captain E E Liebert MC returned from leave to UK and took over command of Company.	
do	9.12.17	do	Church Parade. Sergeant- L.P. Selby admitted to hospital sick	

Army Form C. 2118.

WAR DIARY
or
INTELLIGENCE SUMMARY.
(Erase heading not required.)

Maj.Ref. BELGIUM & FRANCE Month 17

Instructions regarding War Diaries and Intelligence Summaries are contained in F.S. Regs., Part II. and the Staff Manual respectively. Title pages will be prepared in manuscript.

Place	Date	Hour	Summary of Events and Information	Remarks and references to Appendices
STAPLE AREA	10/12/17	8am to 6pm	Route March.	
do	11/12/17	do	Range took Table 6 Patt I Practices 1, 2, & 3	
do	12/12/17	do	Bath Parade	
do	13/12/17	do	Route March. Genl Adams proceeded on leave to PARIS.	
do	14/12/17	do	Company Training. Conference at Brigade H.Q. Commanding Officer	
do	15/12/17	do	Range work (stoppages)	
do	16/12/17	do	Tunnel Parade	
do	17/12/17	do	Route March Read Riot Act Return from PARIS leave	
do	18/12/17	do	Range shoot (Vickers.)	
			The Divisional General visited the area. 2nd Lieut B.J. March returned from M.E. Base and was taken on the strength of the Company	

Army Form C. 2118.

WAR DIARY
or
INTELLIGENCE SUMMARY.

(Erase heading not required.)

M.G.M. Belgium & France Sheet 27

Instructions regarding War Diaries and Intelligence Summaries are contained in F. S. Regs., Part II. and the Staff Manual respectively. Title pages will be prepared in manuscript.

Place	Date	Hour	Summary of Events and Information	Remarks and references to Appendices
STAPLE AREA	19.12.17	8am to 1pm	Xmas Festivities	
do	20.12.17	do	Company Training	
			Lieut. W.H. Keenan proceeded on leave to UK.	
do	21.12.17	do	Company Training	
do	22.12.17	do	Company Training & Route March	
do	23.12.17	do	Church Parade	
do	24.12.17	do	Company Training & Range Work	
do	25.12.17	do	Church Parade	
			Tactical Scheme. Formation of Ammunition Dumps &c	
do	26.12.17	do	Company Training & Range Work	
do	27.12.17	do	Lecture by the Commanding Officer	
do	28.12.17	do	Route March	

(A7092). Wt W2839/M1293. 75,000. 1/17. D. D. & L., Ltd. Forms/C.2118/14.

WAR DIARY
or
INTELLIGENCE SUMMARY.

Army Form C. 2118.

Belgium & France
Week 27

Place	Date	Hour	Summary of Events and Information	Remarks and references to Appendices
STAPLE AREA	29.12.17	8am to 6pm	Company training. Checking of Equipment. Field "Palaver" admitted 15 hospital sick (115 C.C.S.) Church Parade	
do	30.12.17	do	Company training. Range Work	
do	31.12.17	do	Strength of Company Officers 10 Other Ranks 92 Total 102	

1.1.1918

O.E. Osbert, Captain
Commanding 202nd W.G. Coy

202
MACHINE GUN COMPANY

Jan 1918.

Army Form C. 2118.

WAR DIARY
or
INTELLIGENCE SUMMARY

(Erase heading not required.)

202 M E Coy
Vol 11

MAP REF:
Belgium France Sheet 27

Instructions regarding War Diaries and Intelligence Summaries are contained in F. S. Regs., Part II. and the Staff Manual respectively. Title Pages will be prepared in manuscript.

Place	Date	Hour	Summary of Events and Information	Remarks and references to Appendices
STAPLE AREA	1-1-19	8 am 8 pm	Strength of Company. Officers 10 OR 171 Totals 181. Company moved from billets at U.18.f.2.1 to U.10 to T.1.2.	
do	2.1.18	do	Camp fatigues	
do	3.1.18	do	Company Training (Sections 1+2 Range Work) (3+4 Route March.)	
do	4.1.18	do	Company Training (Sections 3+4 Range Work) (1+2 Route March)	
do	5.1.18	do	Company Training	
do	6.1.18	do	Church Parade	
do	7.1.18	do	Route March	

Army Form C. 2118.

WAR DIARY
or
INTELLIGENCE SUMMARY

(Erase heading not required.)

MAP REF.
BELGIUM & FRANCE Sheet 27/28
ZONNEBEKE Sheet 28 N.E.

Instructions regarding War Diaries and Intelligence Summaries are contained in F. S. Regs., Part II. and the Staff Manual respectively. Title Pages will be prepared in manuscript.

Place	Date	Hour	Summary of Events and Information	Remarks and references to Appendices
STAPLE AREA.	8-1-18	8 am	Company training.	
Do.	9-1-18	8 am	Cleaning & Packing Limbers.	
STAPLE AREA.	10-1-18	5-	Transport moved off at 6.30 am to WIPPENHOEK en route for CANAL AREA. Baths.	
	11-1-18	5-	Company moved from STAPLE AREA by bus from LONGUE CROIX (HONDEGHEM) and took over billets at H.18.c.40.20 (CANAL AREA)	
CANAL AREA & ZONNEBEKE SECTOR	12-1-18	5-	202 Machine Gun Coy relieved 254 M. G. Coy in the line	
Do.	13-1-18	5-	"Details" and Transport took over camp and lines at H.18.c.5.2 vacated by 254 M.G. Coy.	
Do.	14-1-18	5-	Improving Machine Gun positions in the line. "Details" on Camp fatigues, cleaning & checking guns, etc.	

MAP REF.
BELGIUM & FRANCE Sheet 28.
ZONNEBEKE Sheet 28 N.E.

Army Form C. 2118.

WAR DIARY
or
INTELLIGENCE SUMMARY.
(Erase heading not required.)

Instructions regarding War Diaries and Intelligence Summaries are contained in F. S. Regs., Part II. and the Staff Manual respectively. Title pages will be prepared in manuscript.

Place	Date	Hour	Summary of Events and Information	Remarks and references to Appendices
ZONNEBEKE SECTOR & CANAL AREA	15.1.18	8am to 8am	New M.G. positions selected in accordance with Corps Defence Scheme. "Details on Camp Improvements"	
Do	16.1.18	Do	202 M.G. Coy relieved 4 guns of 203 M.G. Coy in the front line positions, Nos. 85, 86, 87 & 88.	
Do	17.1.18	Do	Construction of new emplacements and dugouts. Details on Camp Improvements.	
Do	18.1.18	Do	Construction of new emplacements and dugouts. Details on Camp Improvements.	
Do	19.1.18	Do	202 M.G. Coy. relieved 4 guns of the 203rd M.G. Coy at "C" Battery position. 2nd Lieut. R.L.B. WATTS reported his arrival from the M.G.C. Base Depot.	
Do	20.1.18	Do	O.C. 202 M.G. Coy moved from RIGHT COY. H.Q. (RIGHT SUB-SECTOR) to LEFT COY. H.Q. (LEFT SUB-SECTOR)	
Do	21.1.18	Do	Selection of new Machine Gun positions in accordance with scheme suggested by D.M.G.O., 66th Division.	

Army Form C. 2118.

WAR DIARY
or
INTELLIGENCE SUMMARY

(Erase heading not required.)

MAP REF. BELGIUM FRANCE Sheet 28
ZONNEBEKE Sheet 28 N.E.

Place	Date	Hour	Summary of Events and Information	Remarks and references to Appendices
ZONNE-BEKE SECTOR & CHMAL AREA	22.1.18	8am to 8am	Construction of new Emplacements at B New Zealand M.G.Cy. relieved 4 guns of 203 M.G.Cy from "A" Battery position (J.3.d.30.90)	
	23.1.18	S	Construction of new Emplacements and dug-outs. "Details" on Camp fatigues & improvements	
	24.1.18	S	Construction of new Emplacements and dug-outs. Inter-section reliefs. "Details" improving Horse Standings	
	25.1.18	S	Construction of new Emplacements and dug-outs. "Details" on Camp improvements & Horse Standings	
	26.1.18	S	Construction of new Emplacements & dug-outs. A few rounds were fired at K.A. which attempted to cross our lines. Inter-section relief. "Details" on Camp Improvements & Horse Standings	

WAR DIARY or INTELLIGENCE SUMMARY

Army Form C. 2118.

MAP REF:
BELGIUM & FRANCE Sheet 28
ZONNEBEKE Sheet 28 N.E.

Place	Date	Hour	Summary of Events and Information	Remarks and references to Appendices
ZONNEBEKE SECTOR & CANAL AREA	27.1.18	2 am to 6 am	Construction of new emplacements & dugouts. G.O.C. visited "C" Battery position. 250 rounds were fired at E.A. Baths for "Details".	
Do	28.1.18	Do	Construction of new emplacements & dug-outs. Enemy obtained a direct hit on one of our gun emplacements, destroying the gun & tripod, and slightly wounding one of the team.	
Do	29.1.18	Do	Construction of new emplacements and dug-outs. Inter-section relief. Details cleaning guns & checking gun equipment.	
Do	30.1.18	Do	Construction of new emplacements & dug-outs. "Details" on Camp improvements.	
Do	31.1.18	Do	Emplacements & dug-outs completed. New positions occupied, & belt of fire of Guns in accordance with Corps Defence Scheme.	

Strength of Company.

Officers. 10
Other Ranks. 175
Total. 185

G.F. Gybert, Captain
Comdg. 202 M.G. Coy.

1-2-1918.

CONFIDENTIAL

WAR DIARY

OF

202 MACHINE GUN Coy

FROM FEBY 1st TO FEBY 28th 1918.

Army Form C. 2118.

WAR DIARY
or
INTELLIGENCE SUMMARY.
(Erase heading not required.)

FRANCE Sheets 27 & 28 ROSIERES Sector CANAL AREA

Instructions regarding War Diaries and Intelligence Summaries are contained in F. S. Regs., Part II. and the Staff Manual respectively. Title pages Continued Sheet will be prepared in manuscript.

Place	Date	Hour	Summary of Events and Information	Remarks and references to Appendices
ZONNEBEKE SECTOR & CANAL AREA	1.2.18	8 AM	Strength of Company. Officers 10, O.Ranks 175, Total 185	
do	2.2.18	8 AM	Improving Gun Positions & Transport Lines	
do	3.2.18	do	Improving Gun Positions & Transport Lines continued. Capt G.E. Lucerne reported from M to Kenny at CHALONS. Lieut Witterdin took over command of Coy.	
do	4.2.18	do	Work on Gun Positions & Transport Lines continued. One gun prevented an hostile aeroplane from crossing our lines.	
do	5.2.18	do	Continuation of work on Gun Positions and Transport Line. Lieut P McPhee reported from M. S Base and was taken on strength of the Company. An hostile aeroplane was driven back by our guns.	
do	6.2.18	do	Continuation of work on improving of gun positions and transport lines	

FRANCE Note 27/1/18
ROSIERES
o Combles

WAR DIARY
or
INTELLIGENCE SUMMARY.

Army Form C. 2118.

(Erase heading not required.)

Place	Date	Hour	Summary of Events and Information	Remarks and references to Appendices
ZONNEBEKE SECTOR & CANAL AREA	7.2.18	8AM to 8AM	Improving of Reserve & Transport Lines continued.	
do	8.2.18	do	4 Guns of the 149th Machine Gun Company relieved on 4 guns at "C" Battery Position. The remainder of Guns carried on with improving gun positions	
do	9.2.18	do	Construction of work on Gun Position and Transport Lines. 8/9/18 Guns of the 240th Machine Gun Company relieved ours on 2 guns at Position No. 86, 87.	
do	10.2.18	do	Our Guns at No. 58, 59, 90 Positions were withdrawn in accordance with instructions received from Brigade. 4 Guns remained in Tonight. Coys and proceeded to the New Area sold 199 Infantry Brigade on 12.2.18	

Army Form C. 2118.

WAR DIARY
or
INTELLIGENCE SUMMARY.

(Erase heading not required.)

SUM FRANCE Sheets 27 & 28 & ROSIERES + Continued Sheet

Instructions regarding War Diaries and Intelligence Summaries are contained in F. S. Regs., Part II. and the Staff Manual respectively. Title pages will be prepared in manuscript.

Place	Date	Hour	Summary of Events and Information	Remarks and references to Appendices
PROVEN AREA	10.2.18	8 AM to 8 AM	The Company less 3 gun teams marched to PROVEN AREA and took over billets at ROAD CAMP ST JAN-TER-BIEZEN F2SC.	
do	11.2.18	do	Checking of Gun Equipment. Back Parade Company Gunnery Drills. 3 Gun teams who not relieved until 10.2.18 rejoined the company	
do	12.2.18	do	Company Training	
do	13.2.18	do	Company Training	
do	14.2.18	do	Tarewell Parade to 76 & 75 Coy Two	
do	15.2.18	do	Packing limbers ready for move. 76 Company	
do	16.2.18	do	Marched to PROVEN STATION and entrained for GUILLAUCOURT. Detrained at GUILLAU COURT at 12.30 a.m took over billets at W14a 9.0	

War Diary ROSIERES Comprehensive Sheet

Army Form C. 2118.

WAR DIARY
or
INTELLIGENCE SUMMARY.
(Erase heading not required.)

Instructions regarding War Diaries and Intelligence Summaries are contained in F. S. Regs., Part II. and the Staff Manual respectively. Title pages will be prepared in manuscript.

Place	Date	Hour	Summary of Events and Information	Remarks and references to Appendices
GUILLAUCOURT	17.2.18	8 AM to 8 AM	Unpacking & Linden.	
do	18.2.18	do	Company having Recreation	
do	19.2.18	do	Company training & Recreation	
do	20.2.18	do	Company training & Recreation	
do	21.2.18	do	Company training & Recreation	
do	22.2.18	do	Route March	
do	23.2.18	do	Company having 1 section co-operates in a Tactical Scheme with 2/1 Bn Two	
do	24.2.18	do	Church Parade	
do	25.2.18	do	The company co-operated with 197 Inf Bde in a Tactical Scheme	

Army Form C. 2118.

Ref ROSIERES Commandant

WAR DIARY
or
INTELLIGENCE SUMMARY.

(Erase heading not required.)

Place	Date	Hour	Summary of Events and Information	Remarks and references to Appendices
CAULAINCOURT	26.1.18	9 AM to 1 PM	Company having Capt. G.E. Oldest M.C. returned from his Course and took over command of Company	
do	27.1.18	do	Getting ready for move	
do	28.1.18	do	The Company marched to VILLERS CARBONNEL and took up billets at STAGING CAMP	
			Strength of Company Officers 11 Other Ranks 172 Total 183	

G. E. Oldest Captain
Commanding 201 M.G. Coy